THE TRIATHLETE'S
Journal

Name _____

Age _____

Year _____

FREE GIFT!

As a thank you for purchasing **The Triathlete's Training Journal**, we would like to give you access to our **ATHLETE PERFORMANCE HUB** part of our website.

In here you will find drills, workouts and exercises in all 3 disciplines of the triathlon.

The sessions are all delivered on video and focus on developing the essential skills in each of swim, bike and run.

We have put these together to help you with your training. Many of our Beckworth Racing athletes have these very sessions included as part of their weekly training schedule.

I hope you enjoy! To Access Your Free Gift, please **visit:**
https://www.beckworthracing.com/training-journal

ATHLETE PERFORMANCE HUB

TRIATHLETE'S *Journal* SECTIONS

01 **Performance Goals**

Write down your goals for the next 6 Months

02 **Training Logbook**

Record your training sessions and details

03 **Race Logbook**

Write further details of your performance at race's you compete in to keep a record for future reference

04 **Messages, Notes and Photos**

Gather messages and photos from training and events

THE TRIATHLETE'S JOURNAL

01

TRIATHLON GOALS

01
6 MONTH TRAINING GOALS

GOAL 1
....
....
....

GOAL 2
....
....
....

GOAL 3
....
....
....

GOAL 4
....
....
....

RACE/COMPETITION GOALS

GOAL 1 ....

GOAL 2 ....

GOAL 3 ....

THE TRIATHLETE'S JOURNAL

02
TRAINING LOGBOOK

TRAINING SESSION LOGBOOK

Date: / /   **Start time** :

End time :

Location ....

Session Completed   SWIM ○   BIKE ○   RUN ○

Weather Conditions   TEMP ☐   ☀ ⛈ ☁ ⛅

Details of the Session   Write down information or details about your training session including distances, times to record, how you felt, equipment issues or other aspects of your session.

....
....
....
....
....
....
....

Total Distance Covered: SWIM _____   BIKE _____   RUN _____

Coach Feedback   Write down if your coach provided any feedback, information or discussed technique or other focus areas.

....
....
....

Other Details   Record your weight, sleeping patterns, how you are feeling, other cross training you may be doing etc..

....
....
....

Next Scheduled session   Day: _____   Time : _____   AM/PM

Location ....

TRAINING SESSION LOGBOOK

Date: / /

Start time :

End time :

Location ....

Session Completed   SWIM   BIKE   RUN

Weather Conditions   TEMP   ☀   🌧   ☁   🌤

Details of the Session   Write down information or details about your training session including distances, times to record, how you felt, equipment issues or other aspects of your session.

....
....
....
....
....
....
....

Total Distance Covered: SWIM   BIKE   RUN

Coach Feedback   Write down if your coach provided any feedback, information or discussed technique or other focus areas.

....
....
....

Other Details   Record your weight, sleeping patterns, how you are feeling, other cross training you may be doing etc..

....
....
....

Next Scheduled session   Day: Time   :   AM/PM

Location ....

TRAINING SESSION LOGBOOK

Date: / /   **Start time** :

End time :

Location ....

Session Completed   SWIM   BIKE   RUN

Weather Conditions   TEMP

Details of the Session   Write down information or details about your training session including distances, times to record, how you felt, equipment issues or other aspects of your session.

....
....
....
....
....
....
....

Total Distance Covered: SWIM   BIKE   RUN

Coach Feedback   Write down if your coach provided any feedback, information or discussed technique or other focus areas.

....
....
....

Other Details   Record your weight, sleeping patterns, how you are feeling, other cross training you may be doing etc..

....
....
....

Next Scheduled session   Day: Time   :   AM/PM

Location ....

TRAINING SESSION LOGBOOK

Date: / /   **Start time** :

End time :

Location ....

Session Completed   SWIM   BIKE   RUN

Weather Conditions   TEMP

Details of the Session   Write down information or details about your training session including distances, times to record, how you felt, equipment issues or other aspects of your session.

....
....
....
....
....
....
....

Total Distance Covered: SWIM   BIKE   RUN

Coach Feedback   Write down it your coach provided any feedback, information or discussed technique or other focus areas.

....
....
....

Other Details   Record your weight, sleeping patterns, how you are feeling, other cross training you may be doing etc..

....
....
....

Next Scheduled session   Day: Time :   AM/PM

Location ....

TRAINING SESSION LOGBOOK

Date: / / **Start time** :

End time :

Location ....

Session Completed   SWIM   BIKE   RUN

Weather Conditions   TEMP   ☀   🌧   ☁   ⛅

Details of the Session   Write down information or details about your training session including distances, times to record, how you felt, equipment issues or other aspects of your session.

....
....
....
....
....
....

Total Distance Covered: SWIM   BIKE   RUN

Coach Feedback   Write down if your coach provided any feedback, information or discussed technique or other focus areas.

....
....

Other Details   Record your weight, sleeping patterns, how you are feeling, other cross training you may be doing etc..

....
....
....

Next Scheduled session   Day: Time   :   AM/PM

Location ....

TRAINING SESSION LOGBOOK

Date: / /   **Start time** :

End time :

Location ....

Session Completed   SWIM   BIKE   RUN

Weather Conditions   TEMP   ☀ ☔ ☁ ⛅

Details of the Session   Write down information or details about your training session including distances, times to record, how you felt, equipment issues or other aspects of your session.

....
....
....
....
....
....
....

Total Distance Covered: SWIM   BIKE   RUN

Coach Feedback   Write down if your coach provided any feedback, information or discussed technique or other focus areas.

....
....
....

Other Details   Record your weight, sleeping patterns, how you are feeling, other cross training you may be doing etc..

....
....
....

Next Scheduled session   Day: Time :   AM/PM

Location ....

TRAINING SESSION LOGBOOK

Date: / / **Start time** :

End time :

Location ....

Session Completed SWIM BIKE RUN

Weather Conditions TEMP

Details of the Session Write down information or details about your training session including distances, times to record, how you felt, equipment issues or other aspects of your session.

....
....
....
....
....
....

Total Distance Covered: SWIM BIKE RUN

Coach Feedback Write down if your coach provided any feedback, information or discussed technique or other focus areas.

....
....
....

Other Details Record your weight, sleeping patterns, how you are feeling, other cross training you may be doing etc..

....
....
....

Next Scheduled session Day: Time : AM/PM

Location ....

7 SESSION REFLECTION

Date: /   /

Total training time for past 7 sessions: HRS   MINS

Total distance covered for each discipline:

SWIM   BIKE   RUN

Overall, my training sessions for the past 7 days have been:

Excellent   Very Good   Good   Poor

Feedback/Notes From Sessions

....
....
....
....

Other Details   How are you feeling? Is your training progressing as planned? Have you specific goals you wish to achieve for your next 7 training sessions?

....
....
....
....
....
....
....
....

TRAINING SESSION LOGBOOK

Date: / / **Start time** :

 End time :

Location ....

Session Completed SWIM BIKE RUN

Weather Conditions TEMP ☀ ⛈ ☁ ⛅

Details of the Session Write down information or details about your training session including distances, times to record, how you felt, equipment issues or other aspects of your session.

....
....
....
....
....
....

Total Distance Covered: SWIM BIKE RUN

Coach Feedback Write down if your coach provided any feedback, information or discussed technique or other focus areas.

....
....
....

Other Details Record your weight, sleeping patterns, how you are feeling, other cross training you may be doing etc..

....
....
....

Next Scheduled session Day: Time : AM/PM

Location ....

TRAINING SESSION LOGBOOK

Date: / /   **Start time** :

End time :

Location ....

Session Completed   SWIM   BIKE   RUN

Weather Conditions   TEMP   ☀ 🌧 ☁ ⛅

Details of the Session   Write down information or details about your training session including distances, times to record, how you felt, equipment issues or other aspects of your session.

....
....
....
....
....
....
....

Total Distance Covered: SWIM   BIKE   RUN

Coach Feedback   Write down if your coach provided any feedback, information or discussed technique or other focus areas.

....
....
....

Other Details   Record your weight, sleeping patterns, how you are feeling, other cross training you may be doing etc..

....
....
....

Next Scheduled session   Day: Time : AM/PM

Location ....

TRAINING SESSION LOGBOOK

Date: /   /   **Start time**   :

End time   :

Location ....

Session Completed   SWIM   BIKE   RUN

Weather Conditions   TEMP

Details of the Session   Write down information or details about your training session including distances, times to record, how you felt, equipment issues or other aspects of your session.

....
....
....
....
....
....

Total Distance Covered: SWIM   BIKE   RUN

Coach Feedback   Write down if your coach provided any feedback, information or discussed technique or other focus areas.

....
....
....

Other Details   Record your weight, sleeping patterns, how you are feeling, other cross training you may be doing etc..

....
....
....

Next Scheduled session   Day: Time   :   AM/PM

Location ....

TRAINING SESSION LOGBOOK

Date: / /   **Start time** :

End time :

Location ....

Session Completed   SWIM   BIKE   RUN

Weather Conditions   TEMP

Details of the Session   Write down information or details about your training session including distances, times to record, how you felt, equipment issues or other aspects of your session.

....
....
....
....
....
....
....

Total Distance Covered: SWIM   BIKE   RUN

Coach Feedback   Write down if your coach provided any feedback, information or discussed technique or other focus areas.

....
....
....

Other Details   Record your weight, sleeping patterns, how you are feeling, other cross training you may be doing etc..

....
....
....

Next Scheduled session   Day: Time :   AM/PM

Location ....

TRAINING SESSION LOGBOOK

Date: /   /   **Start time**   :

                          End time   :

Location ....

Session Completed   SWIM   BIKE   RUN

Weather Conditions   TEMP   ☀️ 🌧️ ☁️ ⛅

Details of the Session   Write down information or details about your training session including distances, times to record, how you felt, equipment issues or other aspects of your session.

....
....
....
....
....
....

Total Distance Covered: SWIM   BIKE   RUN

Coach Feedback   Write down if your coach provided any feedback, information or discussed technique or other focus areas.

....
....
....

Other Details   Record your weight, sleeping patterns, how you are feeling, other cross training you may be doing etc..

....
....
....

Next Scheduled session   Day: Time   :   AM/PM

Location ....

TRAINING SESSION LOGBOOK

Date: / / **Start time** :

 End time :

Location ....

Session Completed SWIM BIKE RUN

Weather Conditions TEMP

Details of the Session Write down information or details about your training session including distances, times to record, how you felt, equipment issues or other aspects of your session.

....
....
....
....
....
....

Total Distance Covered: SWIM BIKE RUN

Coach Feedback Write down if your coach provided any feedback, information or discussed technique or other focus areas.

....
....
....

Other Details Record your weight, sleeping patterns, how you are feeling, other cross training you may be doing etc..

....
....
....

Next Scheduled session Day: Time : AM/PM

Location ....

TRAINING SESSION LOGBOOK

Date: / / **Start time** :

End time :

Location ....

Session Completed   SWIM   BIKE   RUN

Weather Conditions   TEMP

Details of the Session   Write down information or details about your training session including distances, times to record, how you felt, equipment issues or other aspects of your session.

....
....
....
....
....
....

Total Distance Covered: SWIM   BIKE   RUN

Coach Feedback   Write down if your coach provided any feedback, information or discussed technique or other focus areas.

....
....

Other Details   Record your weight, sleeping patterns, how you are feeling, other cross training you may be doing etc..

....
....
....

Next Scheduled session   Day: Time   :   AM/PM

Location ....

7 SESSION REFLECTION

Date: / /

Total training time for past 7 sessions: HRS   MINS

Total distance covered for each discipline:

SWIM   BIKE   RUN

Overall, my training sessions for the past 7 days have been:

Excellent   Very Good   Good   Poor

Feedback/Notes From Sessions

....
....
....
....

Other Details   How are you feeling? Is your training progressing as planned? Have you specific goals you wish to achieve for your next 7 training sessions?

....
....
....
....
....
....
....
....

TRAINING SESSION LOGBOOK

Date: /   /   **Start time**   :

End time   :

Location ....

Session Completed   SWIM   BIKE   RUN

Weather Conditions   TEMP

Details of the Session   Write down information or details about your training session including distances, times to record, how you felt, equipment issues or other aspects of your session.

....
....
....
....
....
....

Total Distance Covered: SWIM   BIKE   RUN

Coach Feedback   Write down if your coach provided any feedback, information or discussed technique or other focus areas.

....
....
....

Other Details   Record your weight, sleeping patterns, how you are feeling, other cross training you may be doing etc..

....
....
....

Next Scheduled session   Day: Time   :   AM/PM

Location ....

TRAINING SESSION LOGBOOK

Date: / / **Start time** :

End time :

Location ....

Session Completed SWIM   BIKE   RUN

Weather Conditions TEMP

Details of the Session Write down information or details about your training session including distances, times to record, how you felt, equipment issues or other aspects of your session.

....
....
....
....
....
....
....

Total Distance Covered: SWIM   BIKE   RUN

Coach Feedback Write down if your coach provided any feedback, information or discussed technique or other focus areas.

....
....
....

Other Details Record your weight, sleeping patterns, how you are feeling, other cross training you may be doing etc..

....
....
....

Next Scheduled session Day: Time :   AM/PM

Location ....

TRAINING SESSION LOGBOOK

Date: / /   **Start time** :

End time :

Location ....

Session Completed   SWIM   BIKE   RUN

Weather Conditions   TEMP

Details of the Session   Write down information or details about your training session including distances, times to record, how you felt, equipment issues or other aspects of your session.

....
....
....
....
....
....

Total Distance Covered: SWIM   BIKE   RUN

Coach Feedback   Write down if your coach provided any feedback, information or discussed technique or other focus areas.

....
....
....

Other Details   Record your weight, sleeping patterns, how you are feeling, other cross training you may be doing etc..

....
....
....

Next Scheduled session   Day: Time :   AM/PM

Location ....

TRAINING SESSION LOGBOOK

Date: / /   **Start time** :

End time :

Location ....

Session Completed   SWIM   BIKE   RUN

Weather Conditions   TEMP

Details of the Session   Write down information or details about your training session including distances, times to record, how you felt, equipment issues or other aspects of your session.

....
....
....
....
....
....

Total Distance Covered: SWIM   BIKE   RUN

Coach Feedback   Write down if your coach provided any feedback, information or discussed technique or other focus areas.

....
....
....

Other Details   Record your weight, sleeping patterns, how you are feeling, other cross training you may be doing etc..

....
....
....

Next Scheduled session   Day: Time :   AM/PM

Location ....

TRAINING SESSION LOGBOOK

Date: / /   **Start time** :

End time :

Location ....

Session Completed   SWIM   BIKE   RUN

Weather Conditions TEMP

Details of the Session   Write down information or details about your training session including distances, times to record, how you felt, equipment issues or other aspects of your session.

....
....
....
....
....
....

Total Distance Covered: SWIM   BIKE   RUN

Coach Feedback   Write down if your coach provided any feedback, information or discussed technique or other focus areas.

....
....
....

Other Details   Record your weight, sleeping patterns, how you are feeling, other cross training you may be doing etc..

....
....
....

Next Scheduled session   Day: Time   :   AM/PM

Location ....

TRAINING SESSION LOGBOOK

Date: / /   **Start time** :

End time :

Location ....

Session Completed   SWIM   BIKE   RUN

Weather Conditions   TEMP

Details of the Session   Write down information or details about your training session including distances, times to record, how you felt, equipment issues or other aspects of your session.

....
....
....
....
....
....
....

Total Distance Covered: SWIM   BIKE   RUN

Coach Feedback   Write down if your coach provided any feedback, information or discussed technique or other focus areas.

....
....
....

Other Details   Record your weight, sleeping patterns, how you are feeling, other cross training you may be doing etc..

....
....
....

Next Scheduled session   Day: Time :   AM/PM

Location ....

TRAINING SESSION LOGBOOK

Date: / /   **Start time** :

End time :

Location ....

Session Completed   SWIM   BIKE   RUN

Weather Conditions   TEMP

Details of the Session Write down information or details about your training session including distances, times to record, how you felt, equipment issues or other aspects of your session.

....
....
....
....
....
....

Total Distance Covered: SWIM   BIKE   RUN

Coach Feedback Write down if your coach provided any feedback, information or discussed technique or other focus areas.

....
....

Other Details Record your weight, sleeping patterns, how you are feeling, other cross training you may be doing etc..

....
....

Next Scheduled session   Day: Time   :   AM/PM

Location ....

7 SESSION REFLECTION

Date: / /

Total training time for past 7 sessions: HRS   MINS

Total distance covered for each discipline:

SWIM   BIKE   RUN

Overall, my training sessions for the past 7 days have been:

Excellent   Very Good   Good   Poor

Feedback/Notes From Sessions

....
....
....
....

Other Details   How are you feeling? Is your training progressing as planned? Have you specific goals you wish to achieve for your next 7 training sessions?

....
....
....
....
....
....
....
....

TRAINING SESSION LOGBOOK

Date: /   /   **Start time**   :

End time   :

Location ....

Session Completed   SWIM   BIKE   RUN

Weather Conditions   TEMP

Details of the Session   Write down information or details about your training session including distances, times to record, how you felt, equipment issues or other aspects of your session.

....
....
....
....
....
....

Total Distance Covered: SWIM   BIKE   RUN

Coach Feedback   Write down if your coach provided any feedback, information or discussed technique or other focus areas.

....
....
....

Other Details   Record your weight, sleeping patterns, how you are feeling, other cross training you may be doing etc..

....
....
....

Next Scheduled session   Day: Time   :   AM/PM

Location ....

TRAINING SESSION LOGBOOK

Date: / /   **Start time** :

End time :

Location ....

Session Completed   SWIM   BIKE   RUN

Weather Conditions   TEMP

Details of the Session   Write down information or details about your training session including distances, times to record, how you felt, equipment issues or other aspects of your session.

....
....
....
....
....
....
....

Total Distance Covered: SWIM   BIKE   RUN

Coach Feedback   Write down if your coach provided any feedback, information or discussed technique or other focus areas.

....
....
....

Other Details   Record your weight, sleeping patterns, how you are feeling, other cross training you may be doing etc..

....
....
....

Next Scheduled session   Day: Time :   AM/PM

Location ....

TRAINING SESSION LOGBOOK

Date: /   /   **Start time**   :

End time   :

Location ....

Session Completed   SWIM   ●   BIKE   ●   RUN   ●

Weather Conditions   TEMP ☀ 🌧 ☁ ⛅

Details of the Session   Write down information or details about your training session including distances, times to record, how you felt, equipment issues or other aspects of your session.

....
....
....
....
....
....

Total Distance Covered: SWIM   BIKE   RUN

Coach Feedback   Write down if your coach provided any feedback, information or discussed technique or other focus areas.

....
....
....

Other Details   Record your weight, sleeping patterns, how you are feeling, other cross training you may be doing etc..

....
....
....

Next Scheduled session   Day: Time   :   AM/PM

Location ....

TRAINING SESSION LOGBOOK

Date: / / **Start time** :

End time :

Location ....

Session Completed   SWIM   BIKE   RUN

Weather Conditions   TEMP

Details of the Session   Write down information or details about your training session including distances, times to record, how you felt, equipment issues or other aspects of your session.

....
....
....
....
....
....
....

Total Distance Covered: SWIM   BIKE   RUN

Coach Feedback   Write down if your coach provided any feedback, information or discussed technique or other focus areas.

....
....
....

Other Details   Record your weight, sleeping patterns, how you are feeling, other cross training you may be doing etc..

....
....
....

Next Scheduled session   Day: Time : AM/PM

Location ....

TRAINING SESSION LOGBOOK

Date: / /   **Start time** :

End time :

Location ....

Session Completed   SWIM   BIKE   RUN

Weather Conditions   TEMP

Details of the Session   Write down information or details about your training session including distances, times to record, how you felt, equipment issues or other aspects of your session.

....
....
....
....
....

Total Distance Covered: SWIM   BIKE   RUN

Coach Feedback   Write down if your coach provided any feedback, information or discussed technique or other focus areas.

....
....
....

Other Details   Record your weight, sleeping patterns, how you are feeling, other cross training you may be doing etc..

....
....
....

Next Scheduled session Day: Time :   AM/PM

Location ....

TRAINING SESSION LOGBOOK

Date: / /   **Start time** :

End time :

Location ....

Session Completed   SWIM   BIKE   RUN

Weather Conditions   TEMP

Details of the Session   Write down information or details about your training session including distances, times to record, how you felt, equipment issues or other aspects of your session.

....
....
....
....
....
....
....

Total Distance Covered: SWIM   BIKE   RUN

Coach Feedback   Write down if your coach provided any feedback, information or discussed technique or other focus areas.

....
....
....

Other Details   Record your weight, sleeping patterns, how you are feeling, other cross training you may be doing etc..

....
....
....

Next Scheduled session   Day: Time : AM/PM

Location ....

TRAINING SESSION LOGBOOK

Date: / / **Start time** :

End time :

Location ....

Session Completed   SWIM   BIKE   RUN

Weather Conditions   TEMP   ☀   🌧   ☁   ⛅

Details of the Session   Write down information or details about your training session including distances, times to record, how you felt, equipment issues or other aspects of your session.

....
....
....
....
....
....

Total Distance Covered: SWIM   BIKE   RUN

Coach Feedback   Write down if your coach provided any feedback, information or discussed technique or other focus areas.

....
....

Other Details   Record your weight, sleeping patterns, how you are feeling, other cross training you may be doing etc..

....
....
....

Next Scheduled session   Day: Time   :   AM/PM

Location ....

7 SESSION REFLECTION

Date: / /

Total training time for past 7 sessions: HRS   MINS

Total distance covered for each discipline:

SWIM   BIKE   RUN

Overall, my training sessions for the past 7 days have been:

Excellent   Very Good   Good   Poor

Feedback/Notes From Sessions

....
....
....
....

Other Details   How are you feeling? Is your training progressing as planned? Have you specific goals you wish to achieve for your next 7 training sessions?

....
....
....
....
....
....
....
....

TRAINING SESSION LOGBOOK

Date: /   /

Start time   :

End time   :

Location ....

Session Completed   SWIM   BIKE   RUN

Weather Conditions   TEMP

Details of the Session   Write down information or details about your training session including distances, times to record, how you felt, equipment issues or other aspects of your session.

....
....
....
....
....
....

Total Distance Covered: SWIM   BIKE   RUN

Coach Feedback   Write down if your coach provided any feedback, information or discussed technique or other focus areas.

....
....
....

Other Details   Record your weight, sleeping patterns, how you are feeling, other cross training you may be doing etc..

....
....
....

Next Scheduled session   Day: Time   :   AM/PM

Location ....

TRAINING SESSION LOGBOOK

Date: / /

Start time :

End time :

Location ....

Session Completed SWIM BIKE RUN

Weather Conditions TEMP

Details of the Session Write down information or details about your training session including distances, times to record, how you felt, equipment issues or other aspects of your session.

....
....
....
....
....
....
....

Total Distance Covered: SWIM BIKE RUN

Coach Feedback Write down if your coach provided any feedback, information or discussed technique or other focus areas.

....
....
....

Other Details Record your weight, sleeping patterns, how you are feeling, other cross training you may be doing etc..

....
....
....

Next Scheduled session Day: Time : AM/PM

Location ....

TRAINING SESSION LOGBOOK

Date: / / **Start time** :

End time :

Location ....

Session Completed   SWIM   BIKE   RUN

Weather Conditions   TEMP

Details of the Session   Write down information or details about your training session including distances, times to record, how you felt, equipment issues or other aspects of your session.

....
....
....
....
....
....

Total Distance Covered: SWIM   BIKE   RUN

Coach Feedback   Write down if your coach provided any feedback, information or discussed technique or other focus areas.

....
....

Other Details   Record your weight, sleeping patterns, how you are feeling, other cross training you may be doing etc..

....
....

Next Scheduled session   Day: Time   :   AM/PM

Location ....

TRAINING SESSION LOGBOOK

Date: / /   **Start time** :

End time :

Location ....

Session Completed   SWIM   BIKE   RUN

Weather Conditions   TEMP   ☀ ⛅ ☁ 🌥

Details of the Session   Write down information or details about your training session including distances, times to record, how you felt, equipment issues or other aspects of your session.

....
....
....
....
....
....
....

Total Distance Covered: SWIM   BIKE   RUN

Coach Feedback   Write down if your coach provided any feedback, information or discussed technique or other focus areas.

....
....
....

Other Details   Record your weight, sleeping patterns, how you are feeling, other cross training you may be doing etc..

....
....
....

Next Scheduled session   Day: Time :   AM/PM

Location ....

TRAINING SESSION LOGBOOK

Date: ___ / ___ / ___   **Start time** ___ : ___

End time ___ : ___

Location ....

Session Completed   SWIM ○   BIKE ○   RUN ○

Weather Conditions   TEMP _____   ☀ ⛈ ☁ ⛅

Details of the Session   Write down information or details about your training session including distances, times to record, how you felt, equipment issues or other aspects of your session.

....
....
....
....
....
....
....

Total Distance Covered: SWIM _____   BIKE _____   RUN _____

Coach Feedback   Write down if your coach provided any feedback, information or discussed technique or other focus areas.

....
....
....

Other Details   Record your weight, sleeping patterns, how you are feeling, other cross training you may be doing etc..

....
....
....

Next Scheduled session   Day: _____   Time ___ : ___   AM/PM

Location ....

TRAINING SESSION LOGBOOK

Date: / /   **Start time**   :

End time   :

Location ....

Session Completed   SWIM   BIKE   RUN

Weather Conditions   TEMP

Details of the Session   Write down information or details about your training session including distances, times to record, how you felt, equipment issues or other aspects of your session.

....
....
....
....
....
....
....

Total Distance Covered: SWIM   BIKE   RUN

Coach Feedback   Write down if your coach provided any feedback, information or discussed technique or other focus areas.

....
....
....

Other Details   Record your weight, sleeping patterns, how you are feeling, other cross training you may be doing etc..

....
....
....

Next Scheduled session   Day: Time   :   AM/PM

Location ....

TRAINING SESSION LOGBOOK

Date: / /   **Start time** :

End time :

Location ....

Session Completed   SWIM   BIKE   RUN

Weather Conditions   TEMP   ☀️ 🌧️ ☁️ ⛅

Details of the Session   Write down information or details about your training session including distances, times to record, how you felt, equipment issues or other aspects of your session.

....
....
....
....
....
....

Total Distance Covered: SWIM   BIKE   RUN

Coach Feedback   Write down if your coach provided any feedback, information or discussed technique or other focus areas.

....
....
....

Other Details   Record your weight, sleeping patterns, how you are feeling, other cross training you may be doing etc..

....
....
....

Next Scheduled session   Day: Time   :   AM/PM

Location ....

7 SESSION REFLECTION

Date: /   /

Total training time for past 7 sessions: HRS   MINS

Total distance covered for each discipline:

SWIM   BIKE   RUN

Overall, my training sessions for the past 7 days have been:

Excellent   Very Good   Good   Poor

Feedback/Notes From Sessions

....
....
....
....

Other Details — How are you feeling? Is your training progressing as planned? Have you specific goals you wish to achieve for your next 7 training sessions?

....
....
....
....
....
....
....
....

TRAINING SESSION LOGBOOK

Date: / / **Start time** :

 End time :

Location ....

Session Completed SWIM BIKE RUN

Weather Conditions TEMP ☀ 🌧 ☁ ⛅

Details of the Session Write down information or details about your training session including distances, times to record, how you felt, equipment issues or other aspects of your session.

....
....
....
....
....
....

Total Distance Covered: SWIM BIKE RUN

Coach Feedback Write down if your coach provided any feedback, information or discussed technique or other focus areas.

....
....

Other Details Record your weight, sleeping patterns, how you are feeling, other cross training you may be doing etc..

....
....
....

Next Scheduled session Day: Time : AM/PM

Location ....

TRAINING SESSION LOGBOOK

Date: / /   **Start time** :

End time :

Location ....

Session Completed   SWIM   BIKE   RUN

Weather Conditions   TEMP   ☀   🌧   ☁   ⛅

Details of the Session   Write down information or details about your training session including distances, times to record, how you felt, equipment issues or other aspects of your session.

....
....
....
....
....
....
....

Total Distance Covered: SWIM   BIKE   RUN

Coach Feedback   Write down if your coach provided any feedback, information or discussed technique or other focus areas.

....
....
....

Other Details   Record your weight, sleeping patterns, how you are feeling, other cross training you may be doing etc..

....
....
....

Next Scheduled session   Day: Time :   AM/PM

Location ....

TRAINING SESSION LOGBOOK

Date: / / **Start time** :

 End time :

Location ....

Session Completed SWIM BIKE RUN

Weather Conditions TEMP

Details of the Session Write down information or details about your training session including distances, times to record, how you felt, equipment issues or other aspects of your session.

....
....
....
....
....
....

Total Distance Covered: SWIM   BIKE   RUN

Coach Feedback Write down if your coach provided any feedback, information or discussed technique or other focus areas.

....
....
....

Other Details Record your weight, sleeping patterns, how you are feeling, other cross training you may be doing etc..

....
....
....

Next Scheduled session Day: Time   :   AM/PM

Location ....

TRAINING SESSION LOGBOOK

Date: /   /   **Start time**   :

End time   :

Location ....

Session Completed   SWIM   BIKE   RUN

Weather Conditions   TEMP

Details of the Session   Write down information or details about your training session including distances, times to record, how you felt, equipment issues or other aspects of your session.

....
....
....
....
....
....
....

Total Distance Covered: SWIM   BIKE   RUN

Coach Feedback   Write down if your coach provided any feedback, information or discussed technique or other focus areas.

....
....
....

Other Details   Record your weight, sleeping patterns, how you are feeling, other cross training you may be doing etc..

....
....
....

Next Scheduled session   Day: Time   :   AM/PM

Location ....

TRAINING SESSION LOGBOOK

Date: / /   **Start time**   :

                        End time   :

Location ....

Session Completed   SWIM   BIKE   RUN

Weather Conditions   TEMP   ☀   🌧   ☁   ⛅

Details of the Session   Write down information or details about your training session including distances, times to record, how you felt, equipment issues or other aspects of your session.

....
....
....
....
....
....

Total Distance Covered: SWIM   BIKE   RUN

Coach Feedback   Write down if your coach provided any feedback, information or discussed technique or other focus areas.

....
....
....

Other Details   Record your weight, sleeping patterns, how you are feeling, other cross training you may be doing etc..

....
....
....

Next Scheduled session   Day: Time   :   AM/PM

Location ....

TRAINING SESSION LOGBOOK

Date: / /   **Start time** :

End time :

Location ....

Session Completed   SWIM   BIKE   RUN

Weather Conditions   TEMP

Details of the Session   Write down information or details about your training session including distances, times to record, how you felt, equipment issues or other aspects of your session.

....
....
....
....
....
....
....

Total Distance Covered: SWIM   BIKE   RUN

Coach Feedback   Write down it your coach provided any feedback, information or discussed technique or other focus areas.

....
....
....

Other Details   Record your weight, sleeping patterns, how you are feeling, other cross training you may be doing etc..

....
....
....

Next Scheduled session   Day: Time :   AM/PM

Location ....

TRAINING SESSION LOGBOOK

Date: / /   **Start time** :

End time :

Location ....

Session Completed   SWIM   BIKE   RUN

Weather Conditions   TEMP

Details of the Session   Write down information or details about your training session including distances, times to record, how you felt, equipment issues or other aspects of your session.

....
....
....
....
....
....

Total Distance Covered: SWIM   BIKE   RUN

Coach Feedback   Write down if your coach provided any feedback, information or discussed technique or other focus areas.

....
....

Other Details   Record your weight, sleeping patterns, how you are feeling, other cross training you may be doing etc..

....
....

Next Scheduled session   Day: Time   :   AM/PM

Location ....

7 SESSION REFLECTION

Date: /   /

Total training time for past 7 sessions: HRS   MINS

Total distance covered for each discipline:

SWIM   BIKE   RUN

Overall, my training sessions for the past 7 days have been:

Excellent   Very Good   Good   Poor

Feedback/Notes From Sessions

....
....
....
....

Other Details   How are you feeling? Is your training progressing as planned? Have you specific goals you wish to achieve for your next 7 training sessions?

....
....
....
....
....
....
....
....

TRAINING SESSION LOGBOOK

Date: / /   **Start time** :

End time :

Location ....

Session Completed   SWIM   BIKE   RUN

Weather Conditions   TEMP   ☀ 🌧 ☁ ⛅

Details of the Session   Write down information or details about your training session including distances, times to record, how you felt, equipment issues or other aspects of your session.

....
....
....
....
....
....

Total Distance Covered: SWIM   BIKE   RUN

Coach Feedback   Write down if your coach provided any feedback, information or discussed technique or other focus areas.

....
....

Other Details   Record your weight, sleeping patterns, how you are feeling, other cross training you may be doing etc..

....
....
....

Next Scheduled session   Day: Time   :   AM/PM

Location ....

TRAINING SESSION LOGBOOK

Date: / /   **Start time** :

End time :

Location ....

Session Completed   SWIM   BIKE   RUN

Weather Conditions   TEMP

Details of the Session   Write down information or details about your training session including distances, times to record, how you felt, equipment issues or other aspects of your session.

....
....
....
....
....
....
....

Total Distance Covered: SWIM   BIKE   RUN

Coach Feedback   Write down if your coach provided any feedback, information or discussed technique or other focus areas.

....
....
....

Other Details   Record your weight, sleeping patterns, how you are feeling, other cross training you may be doing etc..

....
....
....

Next Scheduled session   Day: Time :   AM/PM

Location ....

TRAINING SESSION LOGBOOK

Date: /   /   **Start time**   :

End time   :

Location ....

Session Completed   SWIM ●   BIKE ●   RUN ●

Weather Conditions   TEMP ☀ 🌧 ☁ ⛅

Details of the Session   Write down information or details about your training session including distances, times to record, how you felt, equipment issues or other aspects of your session.

....
....
....
....
....
....
....

Total Distance Covered: SWIM _____   BIKE _____   RUN _____

Coach Feedback   Write down if your coach provided any feedback, information or discussed technique or other focus areas.

....
....
....

Other Details   Record your weight, sleeping patterns, how you are feeling, other cross training you may be doing etc..

....
....
....

Next Scheduled session   Day: Time   :   AM/PM

Location ....

TRAINING SESSION LOGBOOK

Date: / / **Start time** :

End time :

Location ....

Session Completed   SWIM   BIKE   RUN

Weather Conditions   TEMP

Details of the Session   Write down information or details about your training session including distances, times to record, how you felt, equipment issues or other aspects of your session.

....
....
....
....
....
....
....

Total Distance Covered: SWIM   BIKE   RUN

Coach Feedback   Write down if your coach provided any feedback, information or discussed technique or other focus areas.

....
....
....

Other Details   Record your weight, sleeping patterns, how you are feeling, other cross training you may be doing etc..

....
....
....

Next Scheduled session Day: Time   :   AM/PM

Location ....

TRAINING SESSION LOGBOOK

Date: / / **Start time** :

End time :

Location ....

Session Completed   SWIM   BIKE   RUN

Weather Conditions   TEMP   ☀   🌧   ☁   ⛅

Details of the Session   Write down information or details about your training session including distances, times to record, how you felt, equipment issues or other aspects of your session.

....
....
....
....
....
....

Total Distance Covered: SWIM   BIKE   RUN

Coach Feedback   Write down if your coach provided any feedback, information or discussed technique or other focus areas.

....
....
....

Other Details   Record your weight, sleeping patterns, how you are feeling, other cross training you may be doing etc..

....
....
....

Next Scheduled session   Day: Time   :   AM/PM

Location ....

TRAINING SESSION LOGBOOK

Date: / /   **Start time** :

End time :

Location ....

Session Completed   SWIM   BIKE   RUN

Weather Conditions   TEMP

Details of the Session   Write down information or details about your training session including distances, times to record, how you felt, equipment issues or other aspects of your session.

....
....
....
....
....
....
....

Total Distance Covered: SWIM   BIKE   RUN

Coach Feedback   Write down if your coach provided any feedback, information or discussed technique or other focus areas.

....
....
....

Other Details   Record your weight, sleeping patterns, how you are feeling, other cross training you may be doing etc..

....
....
....

Next Scheduled session Day: Time :   AM/PM

Location ....

TRAINING SESSION LOGBOOK

Date: /   /   **Start time**   :

End time   :

Location ....

Session Completed   SWIM ○   BIKE ○   RUN ○

Weather Conditions   TEMP _____ ☀ 🌧 ☁ ⛅

Details of the Session   Write down information or details about your training session including distances, times to record, how you felt, equipment issues or other aspects of your session.

....
....
....
....
....
....
....

Total Distance Covered: SWIM _____ BIKE _____ RUN _____

Coach Feedback   Write down if your coach provided any feedback, information or discussed technique or other focus areas.

....
....

Other Details   Record your weight, sleeping patterns, how you are feeling, other cross training you may be doing etc..

....
....
....

Next Scheduled session   Day: _____   Time _____ : _____   AM/PM

Location ....

7 SESSION REFLECTION

Date: / /

Total training time for past 7 sessions: HRS   MINS

Total distance covered for each discipline:

SWIM   BIKE   RUN

Overall, my training sessions for the past 7 days have been:

Excellent   Very Good   Good   Poor

Feedback/Notes From Sessions

....
....
....
....

Other Details — How are you feeling? Is your training progressing as planned? Have you specific goals you wish to achieve for your next 7 training sessions?

....
....
....
....
....
....
....
....

TRAINING SESSION LOGBOOK

Date: / /   **Start time** :

End time :

Location ....

Session Completed   SWIM   BIKE   RUN

Weather Conditions   TEMP   ☀ 🌧 ☁ ⛅

Details of the Session   Write down information or details about your training session including distances, times to record, how you felt, equipment issues or other aspects of your session.

....
....
....
....
....
....

Total Distance Covered: SWIM   BIKE   RUN

Coach Feedback   Write down if your coach provided any feedback, information or discussed technique or other focus areas.

....
....
....

Other Details   Record your weight, sleeping patterns, how you are feeling, other cross training you may be doing etc..

....
....
....

Next Scheduled session Day: Time :   AM/PM

Location ....

TRAINING SESSION LOGBOOK

Date: / /

Start time :

End time :

Location ....

Session Completed   SWIM   BIKE   RUN

Weather Conditions   TEMP

Details of the Session   Write down information or details about your training session including distances, times to record, how you felt, equipment issues or other aspects of your session.

....
....
....
....
....
....
....

Total Distance Covered: SWIM   BIKE   RUN

Coach Feedback   Write down if your coach provided any feedback, information or discussed technique or other focus areas.

....
....
....

Other Details   Record your weight, sleeping patterns, how you are feeling, other cross training you may be doing etc..

....
....
....

Next Scheduled session   Day: Time : AM/PM

Location ....

TRAINING SESSION LOGBOOK

Date: / /   **Start time** :

End time :

Location ....

Session Completed   SWIM   BIKE   RUN

Weather Conditions   TEMP

Details of the Session   Write down information or details about your training session including distances, times to record, how you felt, equipment issues or other aspects of your session.

....
....
....
....
....
....

Total Distance Covered: SWIM   BIKE   RUN

Coach Feedback   Write down if your coach provided any feedback, information or discussed technique or other focus areas.

....
....

Other Details   Record your weight, sleeping patterns, how you are feeling, other cross training you may be doing etc..

....
....

Next Scheduled session   Day: Time   :   AM/PM

Location ....

TRAINING SESSION LOGBOOK

Date: / /   **Start time** :

End time :

Location ....

Session Completed   SWIM   BIKE   RUN

Weather Conditions   TEMP

Details of the Session   Write down information or details about your training session including distances, times to record, how you felt, equipment issues or other aspects of your session.

....
....
....
....
....
....
....

Total Distance Covered: SWIM   BIKE   RUN

Coach Feedback   Write down if your coach provided any feedback, information or discussed technique or other focus areas.

....
....
....

Other Details   Record your weight, sleeping patterns, how you are feeling, other cross training you may be doing etc..

....
....
....

Next Scheduled session   Day: Time   :   AM/PM

Location ....

TRAINING SESSION LOGBOOK

Date: / / **Start time** :

End time :

Location ....

Session Completed   SWIM   BIKE   RUN

Weather Conditions   TEMP

Details of the Session   Write down information or details about your training session including distances, times to record, how you felt, equipment issues or other aspects of your session.

....
....
....
....
....
....

Total Distance Covered: SWIM   BIKE   RUN

Coach Feedback   Write down if your coach provided any feedback, information or discussed technique or other focus areas.

....
....
....

Other Details   Record your weight, sleeping patterns, how you are feeling, other cross training you may be doing etc..

....
....
....

Next Scheduled session   Day: Time   :   AM/PM

Location ....

TRAINING SESSION LOGBOOK

Date: / /   **Start time** :

End time :

Location ....

Session Completed   SWIM   BIKE   RUN

Weather Conditions   TEMP

Details of the Session   Write down information or details about your training session including distances, times to record, how you felt, equipment issues or other aspects of your session.

....
....
....
....
....
....
....

Total Distance Covered: SWIM   BIKE   RUN

Coach Feedback   Write down if your coach provided any feedback, information or discussed technique or other focus areas.

....
....
....

Other Details   Record your weight, sleeping patterns, how you are feeling, other cross training you may be doing etc..

....
....
....

Next Scheduled session   Day: Time   :   AM/PM

Location ....

TRAINING SESSION LOGBOOK

Date: / / **Start time** :

End time :

Location ....

Session Completed   SWIM ●   BIKE ●   RUN ●

Weather Conditions   TEMP ____   ☀ ☔ ☁ ⛅

Details of the Session   Write down information or details about your training session including distances, times to record, how you felt, equipment issues or other aspects of your session.

....
....
....
....
....
....
....

Total Distance Covered: SWIM _____   BIKE _____   RUN _____

Coach Feedback   Write down if your coach provided any feedback, information or discussed technique or other focus areas.

....
....
....

Other Details   Record your weight, sleeping patterns, how you are feeling, other cross training you may be doing etc..

....
....
....

Next Scheduled session   Day: _____   Time _____ :   AM/PM

Location ....

7 SESSION REFLECTION

Date: / /

Total training time for past 7 sessions: HRS   MINS

Total distance covered for each discipline:

SWIM   BIKE   RUN

Overall, my training sessions for the past 7 days have been:

Excellent   Very Good   Good   Poor

Feedback/Notes From Sessions

....
....
....
....

Other Details — How are you feeling? Is your training progressing as planned? Have you specific goals you wish to achieve for your next 7 training sessions?

....
....
....
....
....
....
....
....

TRAINING SESSION LOGBOOK

Date: / / **Start time** :
              End time :

Location ....

Session Completed   SWIM   BIKE   RUN

Weather Conditions   TEMP   ☀ 🌧 ☁ ⛅

Details of the Session   Write down information or details about your training session including distances, times to record, how you felt, equipment issues or other aspects of your session.

....
....
....
....
....
....

Total Distance Covered: SWIM   BIKE   RUN

Coach Feedback   Write down if your coach provided any feedback, information or discussed technique or other focus areas.

....
....
....

Other Details   Record your weight, sleeping patterns, how you are feeling, other cross training you may be doing etc..

....
....
....

Next Scheduled session   Day: Time :   AM/PM

Location ....

TRAINING SESSION LOGBOOK

Date: / / **Start time** :

End time :

Location ....

Session Completed   SWIM   BIKE   RUN

Weather Conditions   TEMP   ☀ ⛅ ☁ 🌤

Details of the Session   Write down information or details about your training session including distances, times to record, how you felt, equipment issues or other aspects of your session.

....
....
....
....
....
....
....

Total Distance Covered: SWIM   BIKE   RUN

Coach Feedback   Write down it your coach provided any feedback, information or discussed technique or other focus areas.

....
....
....

Other Details   Record your weight, sleeping patterns, how you are feeling, other cross training you may be doing etc..

....
....
....

Next Scheduled session   Day: Time   :   AM/PM

Location ....

TRAINING SESSION LOGBOOK

Date: /   /   **Start time**   :

                                                 End time   :

Location ....

Session Completed   SWIM   BIKE   RUN

Weather Conditions   TEMP   ☀   🌧   ☁   ⛅

Details of the Session   Write down information or details about your training session including distances, times to record, how you felt, equipment issues or other aspects of your session.

....
....
....
....
....
....
....

Total Distance Covered: SWIM   BIKE   RUN

Coach Feedback   Write down if your coach provided any feedback, information or discussed technique or other focus areas.

....
....
....

Other Details   Record your weight, sleeping patterns, how you are feeling, other cross training you may be doing etc..

....
....
....

Next Scheduled session   Day: Time   :   AM/PM

Location ....

TRAINING SESSION LOGBOOK

Date: / /   **Start time** :

End time :

Location ....

Session Completed   SWIM   BIKE   RUN

Weather Conditions   TEMP

Details of the Session   Write down information or details about your training session including distances, times to record, how you felt, equipment issues or other aspects of your session.

....
....
....
....
....
....
....

Total Distance Covered: SWIM   BIKE   RUN

Coach Feedback   Write down it your coach provided any feedback, information or discussed technique or other focus areas.

....
....
....

Other Details   Record your weight, sleeping patterns, how you are feeling, other cross training you may be doing etc..

....
....
....

Next Scheduled session   Day: Time :   AM/PM

Location ....

TRAINING SESSION LOGBOOK

Date: /   /   **Start time**   :

End time   :

Location ....

Session Completed   SWIM   BIKE   RUN

Weather Conditions   TEMP

Details of the Session   Write down information or details about your training session including distances, times to record, how you felt, equipment issues or other aspects of your session.

....
....
....
....
....
....

Total Distance Covered: SWIM   BIKE   RUN

Coach Feedback   Write down if your coach provided any feedback, information or discussed technique or other focus areas.

....
....
....

Other Details   Record your weight, sleeping patterns, how you are feeling, other cross training you may be doing etc..

....
....
....

Next Scheduled session   Day: Time   :   AM/PM

Location ....

TRAINING SESSION LOGBOOK

Date: / /   **Start time** :

End time :

Location ....

Session Completed   SWIM   BIKE   RUN

Weather Conditions   TEMP

Details of the Session   Write down information or details about your training session including distances, times to record, how you felt, equipment issues or other aspects of your session.

....
....
....
....
....
....
....

Total Distance Covered: SWIM   BIKE   RUN

Coach Feedback   Write down if your coach provided any feedback, information or discussed technique or other focus areas.

....
....
....

Other Details   Record your weight, sleeping patterns, how you are feeling, other cross training you may be doing etc..

....
....
....

Next Scheduled session   Day: Time :   AM/PM

Location ....

TRAINING SESSION LOGBOOK

Date: / / **Start time** :

End time :

Location ....

Session Completed SWIM   BIKE   RUN

Weather Conditions TEMP

Details of the Session Write down information or details about your training session including distances, times to record, how you felt, equipment issues or other aspects of your session.

....
....
....
....
....
....

Total Distance Covered: SWIM   BIKE   RUN

Coach Feedback Write down if your coach provided any feedback, information or discussed technique or other focus areas.

....
....

Other Details Record your weight, sleeping patterns, how you are feeling, other cross training you may be doing etc..

....
....

Next Scheduled session Day: Time : AM/PM

Location ....

7 SESSION REFLECTION

Date: /   /

Total training time for past 7 sessions: HRS   MINS

Total distance covered for each discipline:

SWIM   BIKE   RUN

Overall, my training sessions for the past 7 days have been:

Excellent   Very Good   Good   Poor

Feedback/Notes From Sessions

....
....
....
....

Other Details   How are you feeling? Is your training progressing as planned? Have you specific goals you wish to achieve for your next 7 training sessions?

....
....
....
....
....
....
....
....

TRAINING SESSION LOGBOOK

Date: / /   **Start time** :

End time :

Location ....

Session Completed   SWIM   BIKE   RUN

Weather Conditions   TEMP   ☀ ⛅ ☁ 🌤

Details of the Session Write down information or details about your training session including distances, times to record, how you felt, equipment issues or other aspects of your session.

....
....
....
....
....
....

Total Distance Covered: SWIM   BIKE   RUN

Coach Feedback Write down if your coach provided any feedback, information or discussed technique or other focus areas.

....
....
....

Other Details Record your weight, sleeping patterns, how you are feeling, other cross training you may be doing etc..

....
....
....

Next Scheduled session Day: Time   :   AM/PM

Location ....

TRAINING SESSION LOGBOOK

Date: / /   **Start time** :

End time :

Location ....

Session Completed   SWIM   BIKE   RUN

Weather Conditions   TEMP

Details of the Session   Write down information or details about your training session including distances, times to record, how you felt, equipment issues or other aspects of your session.

....
....
....
....
....
....
....

Total Distance Covered: SWIM   BIKE   RUN

Coach Feedback   Write down if your coach provided any feedback, information or discussed technique or other focus areas.

....
....
....

Other Details   Record your weight, sleeping patterns, how you are feeling, other cross training you may be doing etc..

....
....
....

Next Scheduled session   Day: Time :   AM/PM

Location ....

TRAINING SESSION LOGBOOK

Date: /   /   **Start time**   :

End time   :

Location ....

Session Completed   SWIM   BIKE   RUN

Weather Conditions   TEMP

Details of the Session   Write down information or details about your training session including distances, times to record, how you felt, equipment issues or other aspects of your session.

....
....
....
....
....
....

Total Distance Covered: SWIM   BIKE   RUN

Coach Feedback   Write down if your coach provided any feedback, information or discussed technique or other focus areas.

....
....
....

Other Details   Record your weight, sleeping patterns, how you are feeling, other cross training you may be doing etc..

....
....
....

Next Scheduled session   Day: Time   :   AM/PM

Location ....

TRAINING SESSION LOGBOOK

Date: / /   **Start time** :

End time :

Location ....

Session Completed   SWIM   BIKE   RUN

Weather Conditions   TEMP

Details of the Session   Write down information or details about your training session including distances, times to record, how you felt, equipment issues or other aspects of your session.

....
....
....
....
....
....
....

Total Distance Covered: SWIM   BIKE   RUN

Coach Feedback   Write down if your coach provided any feedback, information or discussed technique or other focus areas.

....
....
....

Other Details   Record your weight, sleeping patterns, how you are feeling, other cross training you may be doing etc..

....
....
....

Next Scheduled session   Day: Time :   AM/PM

Location ....

TRAINING SESSION LOGBOOK

Date: / /   **Start time** :

End time :

Location ....

Session Completed   SWIM ○   BIKE ○   RUN ○

Weather Conditions   TEMP ☀ ⛈ ☁ ⛅

Details of the Session   Write down information or details about your training session including distances, times to record, how you felt, equipment issues or other aspects of your session.

....
....
....
....
....
....

Total Distance Covered: SWIM _____ BIKE _____ RUN _____

Coach Feedback   Write down if your coach provided any feedback, information or discussed technique or other focus areas.

....
....
....

Other Details   Record your weight, sleeping patterns, how you are feeling, other cross training you may be doing etc..

....
....
....

Next Scheduled session   Day: _____   Time : _____ AM/PM

Location ....

TRAINING SESSION LOGBOOK

Date: / /   **Start time** :

End time :

Location ....

Session Completed   SWIM   BIKE   RUN

Weather Conditions   TEMP   ☀   ☁🌧   ☁   ⛅

Details of the Session   Write down information or details about your training session including distances, times to record, how you felt, equipment issues or other aspects of your session.

....
....
....
....
....
....
....

Total Distance Covered: SWIM   BIKE   RUN

Coach Feedback   Write down if your coach provided any feedback, information or discussed technique or other focus areas.

....
....
....

Other Details   Record your weight, sleeping patterns, how you are feeling, other cross training you may be doing etc..

....
....
....

Next Scheduled session   Day: Time   :   AM/PM

Location ....

TRAINING SESSION LOGBOOK

Date: /   /

Start time   :

End time   :

Location ....

Session Completed   SWIM   BIKE   RUN

Weather Conditions   TEMP

Details of the Session   Write down information or details about your training session including distances, times to record, how you felt, equipment issues or other aspects of your session.

....

....

....

....

....

....

Total Distance Covered: SWIM   BIKE   RUN

Coach Feedback   Write down if your coach provided any feedback, information or discussed technique or other focus areas.

....

....

....

Other Details   Record your weight, sleeping patterns, how you are feeling, other cross training you may be doing etc..

....

....

....

Next Scheduled session   Day: Time   :   AM/PM

Location ....

7 SESSION REFLECTION

Date: / /

Total training time for past 7 sessions: HRS   MINS

Total distance covered for each discipline:

SWIM   BIKE   RUN

Overall, my training sessions for the past 7 days have been:

Excellent   Very Good   Good   Poor

Feedback/Notes From Sessions

....
....
....
....

Other Details   How are you feeling? Is your training progressing as planned? Have you specific goals you wish to achieve for your next 7 training sessions?

....
....
....
....
....
....
....
....

TRAINING SESSION LOGBOOK

Date: / /   **Start time** :

End time :

Location ....

Session Completed	SWIM	BIKE	RUN
Weather Conditions	TEMP		

Details of the Session   Write down information or details about your training session including distances, times to record, how you felt, equipment issues or other aspects of your session.

....

....

....

....

....

....

Total Distance Covered: SWIM   BIKE   RUN

Coach Feedback   Write down if your coach provided any feedback, information or discussed technique or other focus areas.

....

....

Other Details   Record your weight, sleeping patterns, how you are feeling, other cross training you may be doing etc..

....

....

Next Scheduled session   Day: Time   :   AM/PM

Location ....

TRAINING SESSION LOGBOOK

Date: / /   **Start time** :

End time :

Location ....

Session Completed   SWIM   BIKE   RUN

Weather Conditions   TEMP   ☀ 🌧 ☁ ⛅

Details of the Session   Write down information or details about your training session including distances, times to record, how you felt, equipment issues or other aspects of your session.

....
....
....
....
....
....
....

Total Distance Covered: SWIM   BIKE   RUN

Coach Feedback   Write down if your coach provided any feedback, information or discussed technique or other focus areas.

....
....
....

Other Details   Record your weight, sleeping patterns, how you are feeling, other cross training you may be doing etc..

....
....
....

Next Scheduled session   Day: Time :   AM/PM

Location ....

TRAINING SESSION LOGBOOK

Date: / /   **Start time**   :

End time   :

Location ....

Session Completed   SWIM ○   BIKE ○   RUN ○

Weather Conditions   TEMP ____   ☀ ⛈ ☁ ⛅

Details of the Session   Write down information or details about your training session including distances, times to record, how you felt, equipment issues or other aspects of your session.

....
....
....
....
....
....

Total Distance Covered: SWIM _____   BIKE _____   RUN _____

Coach Feedback   Write down if your coach provided any feedback, information or discussed technique or other focus areas.

....
....
....

Other Details   Record your weight, sleeping patterns, how you are feeling, other cross training you may be doing etc..

....
....
....

Next Scheduled session Day: _____   Time :   AM/PM

Location ....

TRAINING SESSION LOGBOOK

Date: / /   **Start time**   :

End time   :

Location ....

Session Completed   SWIM   BIKE   RUN

Weather Conditions   TEMP   ☀ ☁🌧 ☁ ⛅

Details of the Session   Write down information or details about your training session including distances, times to record, how you felt, equipment issues or other aspects of your session.

....
....
....
....
....
....
....

Total Distance Covered: SWIM   BIKE   RUN

Coach Feedback   Write down if your coach provided any feedback, information or discussed technique or other focus areas.

....
....
....

Other Details   Record your weight, sleeping patterns, how you are feeling, other cross training you may be doing etc..

....
....
....

Next Scheduled session   Day: Time   :   AM/PM

Location ....

TRAINING SESSION LOGBOOK

Date: / /   **Start time** :

End time :

Location ....

Session Completed   SWIM   BIKE   RUN

Weather Conditions   TEMP

Details of the Session   Write down information or details about your training session including distances, times to record, how you felt, equipment issues or other aspects of your session.

....
....
....
....
....
....

Total Distance Covered: SWIM   BIKE   RUN

Coach Feedback   Write down if your coach provided any feedback, information or discussed technique or other focus areas.

....
....

Other Details   Record your weight, sleeping patterns, how you are feeling, other cross training you may be doing etc..

....
....
....

Next Scheduled session   Day: Time   :   AM/PM

Location ....

TRAINING SESSION LOGBOOK

Date: / /   **Start time** :

End time :

Location ....

Session Completed   SWIM   BIKE   RUN

Weather Conditions   TEMP

Details of the Session   Write down information or details about your training session including distances, times to record, how you felt, equipment issues or other aspects of your session.

....
....
....
....
....
....
....

Total Distance Covered: SWIM   BIKE   RUN

Coach Feedback   Write down if your coach provided any feedback, information or discussed technique or other focus areas.

....
....
....

Other Details   Record your weight, sleeping patterns, how you are feeling, other cross training you may be doing etc..

....
....
....

Next Scheduled session   Day: Time   :   AM/PM

Location ....

TRAINING SESSION LOGBOOK

Date: /   /   **Start time**   :

End time   :

Location ....

Session Completed   SWIM   BIKE   RUN

Weather Conditions   TEMP

Details of the Session   Write down information or details about your training session including distances, times to record, how you felt, equipment issues or other aspects of your session.

....
....
....
....
....
....

Total Distance Covered: SWIM   BIKE   RUN

Coach Feedback   Write down if your coach provided any feedback, information or discussed technique or other focus areas.

....
....
....

Other Details   Record your weight, sleeping patterns, how you are feeling, other cross training you may be doing etc..

....
....
....

Next Scheduled session   Day: Time   :   AM/PM

Location ....

7 SESSION REFLECTION

Date: /   /

Total training time for past 7 sessions: HRS   MINS

Total distance covered for each discipline:

SWIM   BIKE   RUN

Overall, my training sessions for the past 7 days have been:

Excellent   Very Good   Good   Poor

Feedback/Notes From Sessions

....
....
....
....

Other Details   How are you feeling? Is your training progressing as planned? Have you specific goals you wish to achieve for your next 7 training sessions?

....
....
....
....
....
....
....
....

03

RACE/EVENT LOGBOOK

RACE LOGBOOK

Date: / /   **Start time** : AM/PM   **Entry Cost:**

Location: ....

Weather Conditions: TEMP

Race Results: What was your time, event placing etc from the event?

....
....
....
....

My Performance:

How was your mindset leading up to the event? How did you feel during stages of the race? What can you take from this event to improve for next time? Was their feedback from a coach, friend or someone else that you should record? Do you have a goal for your next race?

....
....
....
....
....
....
....
....
....
....
....

RACE LOGBOOK

Date: / /   **Start time** : AM/PM   **Entry Cost:**

Location: ....

Weather Conditions: TEMP

Race Results: What was your time, event placing etc from the event?

....
....
....
....

My Performance:

How was your mindset leading up to the event? How did you feel during stages of the race? What can you take from this event to improve for next time? Was their feedback from a coach, friend or someone else that you should record? Do you have a goal for your next race?

....
....
....
....
....
....
....
....
....

RACE LOGBOOK

Date: / / **Start time** : AM/PM **Entry Cost:**

Location: ....

Weather Conditions: TEMP

Race Results: What was your time, event placing etc from the event?

....
....
....
....

My Performance:

How was your mindset leading up to the event? How did you feel during stages of the race? What can you take from this event to improve for next time? Was their feedback from a coach, friend or someone else that you should record? Do you have a goal for your next race?

....
....
....
....
....
....
....
....
....
....
....

RACE LOGBOOK

Date: / /   **Start time** :   AM/PM   **Entry Cost:**

Location: ....

Weather Conditions: TEMP

Race Results: What was your time, event placing etc from the event?

....
....
....
....

My Performance:

How was your mindset leading up to the event? How did you feel during stages of the race? What can you take from this event to improve for next time? Was their feedback from a coach, friend or someone else that you should record? Do you have a goal for your next race?

....
....
....
....
....
....
....
....
....
....

RACE LOGBOOK

Date: / /   **Start time** :   AM/PM   **Entry Cost:**

Location: ....

Weather Conditions: TEMP

Race Results: What was your time, event placing etc from the event?

....
....
....
....

My Performance:

How was your mindset leading up to the event? How did you feel during stages of the race? What can you take from this event to improve for next time? Was their feedback from a coach, friend or someone else that you should record? Do you have a goal for your next race?

....
....
....
....
....
....
....
....
....
....
....

04

Messages, Notes & Photos

Messages & Photo's

Messages & Photo's

Messages & Photo's

Messages & Photo's

Messages & Photo's

JOURNAL NOTES

JOURNAL NOTES

©The Life Graduate Publishing Group

No part of this book may be scanned, reproduced or distributed in any printed or electronic form without the prior permission of the author or publisher.

FREE GIFT!

As a thank you for purchasing **The Triathlete's Training Journal**, we would like to give you access to our **ATHLETE PERFORMANCE HUB** part of our website.

In here you will find drills, workouts and exercises in all 3 disciplines of the triathlon.

The sessions are all delivered on video and focus on developing the essential skills in each of swim, bike and run.

We have put these together to help you with your training. Many of our Beckworth Racing athletes have these very sessions included as part of their weekly training schedule.

I hope you enjoy! To Access Your Free Gift, please **visit:**
https://www.beckworthracing.com/training-journal

THE TRIATHLETE'S
Journal